Nelson English Language Tests
Book 3 Advanced

W S Fowler & Norman Coe

Nelson

Thomas Nelson and Sons Ltd
Nelson House   Mayfield Road
Walton-on-Thames   Surrey
KT12 5PL   UK

51 York Place
Edinburgh
EH1 3JD   UK

Thomas Nelson (Hong Kong) Ltd
Toppan Building 10/F
22A Westlands Road
Quarry Bay   Hong Kong

First published by Thomas Nelson and Sons Ltd 1976
ISBN 0-17-555198-7
NPN 9

Printed in Hong Kong

Acknowledgement
Grateful acknowledgement is due to
Mrs Sonia Brownell Orwell and Secker and
Warburg Ltd, for an extract from *Writers and
Leviathan* by George Orwell.

Contents

Test 350 A

Choose the correct answer. Only one answer is correct.

I had been sitting . .1. . in my usual compartment . .2. . at least ten minutes, waiting . .3. . . The trains from Littlebury never seemed to start . .4. . and I often thought that I could have . .5. . in bed a little longer or had . .6. . cup of tea before . .7. . . Suddenly I heard someone shouting . .8. . the platform outside. A young girl was running towards the train. The man . .9. . put out his hand to stop her but she ran past him and opened the door of my compartment. Then the whistle blew and the train started.

"I nearly missed it, . .10. .?" the girl said. "How long does it take to . .11. . London?"

"It depends on the . .12. ." I said. "Some days it's . .13. . others."

"I'll have to . .14. ., . .15. . late again tomorrow," she said. "It's my first day . .16. . with a new firm today and they told me that the man . .17. . is very strict. I . .18. . him yet so I don't know . .19. . but he sounds a bit frightening."

She talked about her new job . .20. . the way to London and before long, I realised that she was going to work for my firm. My . .21. . secretary had just left so I must be her new boss. . .22. . only fair to tell her.

"Oh, dear," she said. ". .23. . mistake! I wish I . .24. . ."

"Never mind," I said. "At least you'll know when your train's late that. .25. . ."

1 A for myself
   B only myself
   C by myself
   D in my own

2 A for
   B during
   C since
   D meanwhile

3 A the train to start
   B for the train start
   C the train's start
   D for the train to start

4 A on their hour
   B on time
   C at their hour
   D at time

5 A lain
   B laid
   C lied
   D lay

6 A other
   B some other
   C another
   D one other

7 A I had left the home
   B leave from home
   C leaving home
   D to leave home

8 A at
   B by
   C in
   D on

9 A at place
   B on duty
   C for control
   D in post

10 A haven't I
    B don't I
    C wasn't I
    D didn't I

11 A get to
    B arrive to
    C reach to
    D make to

12 A driver to the engine
    B driver engine
    C engine's driver
    D engine driver

13 A far slower that
    B much slower than
    C a lot more slow than
    D a great deal more slow
       that

14 A mend me the watch
    B mend me my watch
    C have my watch
       mended
    D have mended my
       watch

15 A in order not be
    B so as not to be
    C for not being
    D so that it's not

16 A at job
    B in job
    C in work
    D at work

17 A I'm going to work for
    B what I'm going to
       work for
    C for which I'm going
       to work
    D which I'm going to
       work for

18 A didn't meet
    B haven't met
    C didn't know
    D haven't known

19 A what he is like
    B what is he like
    C how he is
    D how is he

20 A through
    B by
    C on
    D in

21 A proper
    B own
    C same
    D self

22 A There was
    B That was
    C It was
    D Was

23 A What a terrible
    B What terrible
    C How terrible
    D So terrible a

24 A had known
    B have known
    C knew
    D would have known

25 A so will the mine be
    B the mine will be, too
    C so will mine
    D mine will be, too

Choose the correct answer. Only one answer is correct.

A Telephone Call

Hello, Mary! I . .26. . you before now but I . .27. . so hard at the office that I didn't have time. My boss . .28. . on holiday tomorrow and he . .29. . arrange everything before he . .30. . If he had given me sensible instructions I could have done the work next week. But you . .31. . the same problems with your boss. Anyway, . .32. . two tickets for the new play at the Grand Theatre on Saturday. . .33. . and see it together?

26 A should have rung
   B must have rung
   C had to ring
   D ought to ring

27 A must work
   B must have worked
   C have had to work
   D ought to work

28 A will go
   B is going
   C shall go
   D shall be going

29 A wants that I
   B would that I
   C would like that I
   D wants me to

30 A leaves
   B shall leave
   C will leave
   D is leaving

31 A have to have
   B can have
   C ought to have
   D must have

32 A they have been given
     to me
   B I have been given
   C I am given
   D they are given to me

33 A May we go
   B Do you like to go
   C Shall we go
   D Will we go

Choose the correct answer. Only one answer is correct.

34 The lift is out of . . . . . so we'll have to walk
 A function   B order   C running   D work

35 Dinner will be ready . . . . . but we have time for a drink before then.
 A currently   B lately   C presently   D suddenly

36 What do you . . . . . to do about the problem now that this solution has failed?
 A attempt   B think   C pretend   D intend

37 We have . . . . . for a new secretary but we haven't had any replies yet.
 A advertised   B advised   C announced   D noticed

38 I've . . . . . for the job and I hope I get it.
 A appointed   B applied   C presented   D succeeded

39 He threw the box out of the window and it fell to the . . . . . outside.
 A flat   B floor   C plain   D ground

40 100 competitors had . . . . . the race.
 A put their names for   B entered for
 C put themselves for   D taken part

41 I'm very . . . . . to you for your help.
 A grateful   B agreeable   C pleased   D thanks

42 He's so mean that he wouldn't give a beggar a . . . . . of bread.

 A peel   B shell   C crust   D skin

43 Will you be able to come to the party? I . . . . . .
 A believe yes   B am afraid not   C don't hope so   D don't expect

44 I never expected you to turn . . . . . at the meeting. I thought you were abroad.
 A around   B on   C in   D up

45 The plane is just going to take . . . . . .
 A away   B out   C off   D up

In this series of questions, three words have the same sound but one does not. Choose the one that does not.

Example: A go   B so   C show   D *do*

46 A knees   B peace   C freeze   D keys

47 A home   B sum   C crumb   D come

48 A straighter   B greater   C water   D later

49 A ache   B shake   C steak   D weak

50 A another   B bother   C brother   D mother

Test 350 B

Choose the correct answer. Only one answer is correct.

I . .1. . don't believe in ghosts . .2. . my experience at the Rose Inn. . .3. . I have never seen one. But ghost stories have made me . .4. . uncomfortable since then. I . .5. . the inn late at night and asked . .6. . .

"There's nothing left," he said, ". .7. . to sleep in Number 7."

"Why not?" I said. "What's wrong with it?" I was so tired that I would have slept . .8. . .

"Nothing," he said slowly. "But something happened there a few months ago."

Every old inn has . .9. . strange stories, so I thought that . .10. . he told me about it, the better. I was willing to listen to anything for . .11. . a bed to sleep in.

"A man came here late at night, . .12. . you," the landlord said. "I thought there was something odd . .13. . him because he kept looking . .14. . his shoulder while he was signing his name in the book. He asked me . .15. . have and I offered . .16. . . ". .17. . a man who has said he'll kill me," he said suddenly. "With a knife." He looked . .18. . that I thought I had better . .19. . him to his room. I locked the door and left him . .20. . . The next day we . .21. . him dead, with a knife beside him. He had . .22. .", the landlord said. "Or someone else had done it. Do you mind sleeping there now you know the story?"

"Well," I said. ". .23. . is following me. But I wish you . .24. . the story in the morning. . .25. . , I'll sleep here on the floor in the bar if you've got a couple of blankets."

1 A already
  B yet
  C no longer
  D still

2 A even though
  B even after
  C although
  D in spite

3 A At least
  B At last
  C At first
  D At once

4 A to feel
  B feel myself
  C feel
  D that I feel

5 A arrived to
  B arrived at
  C reached to
  D reached at

6 A a room of the landlord
  B a room from the landlord
  C the landlord a room
  D the landlord for a room

7 A if you didn't like
  B if you don't like
  C unless you are liking
  D unless you'd like

8 A anywhere
  B somewhere
  C however
  D in whatever place

9 A his
  B its
  C their
  D the

10 A so soon as
B as soon as
C the soonest
D the sooner

11 A the sake of
B the lack of
C the need of
D the wish of

12 A as
B like
C the same that
D similar with

13 A with
B of
C about
D around

14 A through
B back
C over
D after

15 A what room could he
B what room he may
C which room could he
D which room he could

16 A to him the number 7
B to him number 7
C him number 7
D him the number 7

17 A It's
B There's
C That's
D He's

18 A to be so frightened
B so frightened
C with such a fright
D with such fright

19 A to bring
B to take
C bring
D take

20 A by himself
B by his self
C only himself
D in his own

21 A met
B knew
C found
D uncovered

22 A cut himself the throat
B himself cut the throat
C his throat cut
D cut his throat

23 A None
B No one
C Anyone
D Any one

24 A told me
B had told me
C would tell me
D would have told me

25 A As it is
B Like it is
C Being like that
D Being as that

Choose the correct answer. Only one answer is correct.

On the Way to the Seaside

"Darling! There's hardly any petrol left in the tank. I ..26.. it up before we left home. ..27.. a garage quite near but I ..28.. drive carefully until we ..29.. there. If only I ..30.. the petrol before we started out! Damn! I ..31.. this to happen for the last ten minutes. I'll have to push the car to the side of the road because we ..32.. if we leave it here. But I can't imagine what ..33.. to let this happen.

26 A must have filled
   B should have filled
   C would have filled
   D had to fill

27 A There may be
   B It may be
   C There can be
   D It can be

28 A like better
   B would better
   C had better
   D prefer

29 A shall get
   B will get
   C are getting
   D get

30 A checked
   B would have checked
   C had checked
   D have checked

31 A am expecting
   B expect
   C have been expecting
   D was expecting

32 A will be fined
   B will fine
   C will be being fined
   D will be fining

33 A was I thinking about
   B I was thinking about
   C did I think about
   D I thought about

Choose the correct answer. Only one answer is correct.

34 He . . . . . me by two games to one.

    A beat   B conquered   C gained   D won

35 His office is on the third . . . . . of the building.

    A floor   B flat   C ground   D level

36 How long are you thinking of . . . . . in this country?

    A reminding   B staying   C resting   D inhabiting

37 I don't want to go into the sea. I'd rather lie on the . . . . . .

    A coast   B beach   C bank   D seaside

38 I'm . . . . . I didn't pass the examination but I'll do better next time.

    A deceived   B despaired   C disillusioned   D disappointed

39 The lecture was so . . . . . that everyone went to sleep.

    A boring   B bored   C tiring   D tired

40 I . . . . . an answer to my letter within a few days.

    A hope   B wait   C look forward   D expect

41 When he . . . . . he wants to be an architect.

    A ages   B grows   C grows up   D increases

42 It's on the top shelf, out of . . . . . .

    A distance   B reach   C touch   D attempt

43 He's worked so . . . . . that he deserves a rest.

    A roughly   B intensive   C hardly   D hard

44 They're staying with us . . . . . the time being until they find a place of their own.

    A during   B in   C since   D for

45 I'll call . . . . . you at 8.30 and give you a lift to work.

    A in   B for   C at   D up

In this series of questions, three words have the same sound but one does not. Choose the one that does not.

Example: A go   B so   C show   D *do*

46 A blood   B stood   C flood   D mud

47 A word   B third   C stirred   D lord

48 A war   B bar   C far   D star

49 A eyes   B price   C lies   D buys

50 A build   B mild   C wild   D child

Test 350 C

Choose the correct answer. Only one answer is correct.

I can clearly remember the first time I . .1. . Mr Andrews, my old headmaster, . .2. . . .3. . .
During the war, I had been . .4. . school in the north of England but my family had just returned
to London. . .5. . for children to go to and my father had to go from . .6. . , asking them . .7. .
. .8. . pupil. I used to go with him but he had . .9. . hard time trying to persuade people
. .10. . him that I seldom had to do . .11. . . We had been to all the schools . .12. . we lived,
but . .13. . my father argued, the more impossible it became. In the end, we went to a school
. .14. . from home. The headmaster . .15. . for at least an hour. While we were waiting, I
looked round at the . .16. . , . .17. . was one of those old Victorian structures, completely
. .18. . but still standing. I could hear the boys playing in the playground outside. When the
headmaster's secretary finally let us . .19. . his office, Mr Andrews spoke to me first. "Why
do you want to come here?" he said. I had been thinking . .20. . something about studying
but I couldn't help . .21. . the boys outside. "I don't know . .22. . in London," I said. "I'd
like . .23. . with the other boys. I read a lot of books, too" I added. "All right," Mr Andrews
said. "We have one place free, . .24. . ."

My two years at that school were among the . .25. . of my life.

1 A met
  B knew
  C found
  D discovered

2 A even
  B nevertheless
  C although
  D in spite

3 A it's now since over 20
    years
  B it's over 20 years ago
    now
  C it's since more than 20
    years now
  D it makes more than 20
    years now

4 A in the
  B in
  C at
  D at the

5 A There were not
    enough schools left
  B There were not still
    enough schools
  C There did not stay
    enough schools
  D Not enough schools
    rested

6 A one to another
  B each to other
  C one to other
  D the ones to the others

7 A that they took me
  B for taking me
  C for to take me
  D to take me

8 A as
  B as a
  C like
  D like a

12

9 A such
   B such a
   C so
   D a so

10 A just for seeing
   B just for to see
   C even seeing
   D even to see

11 A no test
   B one test
   C any tests
   D some tests

12 A near where
   B near
   C near to
   D near the place there

13 A the most
   B the more
   C how much
   D for how much

14 A at five miles
   B five miles long
   C about five miles away
   D about five miles far

15 A kept us to wait
   B kept us waiting
   C made us to wait
   D made us waiting

16 A building of the school
   B building school
   C school's building
   D school building

17 A which
   B that
   C what
   D it

18 A of the old time
   B outside its time
   C past its date
   D out of date

19 A to enter
   B to pass in
   C to come into
   D into

20 A of saying
   B to say
   C of telling
   D to tell

21 A to remember
   B remembering
   C to remind
   D reminding

22 A no one
   B none
   C someone
   D anyone

23 A that I played
   B the play
   C to play
   D playing

24 A in truth
   B it's the truth
   C in fact
   D it's a fact

25 A happier
   B happiest
   C more happy
   D most happy

Choose the correct answer. Only one answer is correct.

Asking a Next-door Neighbour for Help

Excuse me, Mrs Jones. Would you mind . . 26 . . me a favour? I . . 27 . . shopping. But as soon as I shut my front door I realised I had left my key in the house. So when I . . 28 . . back I . . 29 . . get in. It was very silly of me. I . . 30 . . at all because all the groceries . . 31 . . . I only wanted some mustard. . . 32 . . come in and climb over the fence into my back garden? That's very kind of you. I wish I . . 33 . . give you so much trouble.

26 A making
B doing
C to make
D to do

27 A have just been
B have just gone
C would just go
D was just going

28 A get
B am getting
C shall get
D will get

29 A can't
B will not be able to
C have not been able to
D couldn't

30 A needn't have come out
B didn't need to come out
C mustn't have come out
D hadn't to come out

31 A have already been delivered
B already have been delivered
C are being delivered already
D already are being delivered

32 A Shall I
B Will I
C May I
D Do you want me to

33 A don't have to
B haven't to
C hadn't to
D didn't have to

Choose the correct answer. Only one answer is correct.

34 Would you . . . . . holding this box for me while I open the door?
   A like   B matter   C mind   D object

35 He is . . . . . dark glasses to protect his eyes from the sun.
   A carrying   B fitting   C bearing   D wearing

36 He was told to get off the bus because he couldn't pay the . . . . . .
   A bill   B journey   C travel   D fare

37 They have put the bird in a cage to . . . . . it from flying away.
   A avoid   B prevent   C hinder   D resist

38 He has some very . . . . . habits. He always has a bath with his clothes on.
   A strange   B rare   C uneven   D foreign

39 The . . . . . outside the house said "Private".
   A advice   B label   C notice   D signal

40 If the boss sees you doing that, you'll get into . . . . . .
   A trouble   B nuisance   C mess   D problem

41 I was so . . . . . by the news that I didn't know what to say.
   A admired   B marvelled   C amazed   D wondered

42 He's . . . . . because he has won the prize.
   A nervous   B satisfying   C excited   D exciting

43 He likes lying in bed. He still wasn't . . . . . when I rang him at 10 o'clock.
   A out   B away   C up   D in

44 If you don't know how to spell a word, look it . . . . . in the dictionary.
   A up   B after   C out   D for

45 He carries . . . . . as if he were the boss.
   A through   B off   C out   D on

In this series of questions, three words have the same sound but one does not. Choose the one that does not.

Example: A go   B so   C show   D *do*

46 A dull   B bull   C wool   D pull

47 A earth   B birth   C worth   D north

48 A gone   B none   C won   D son

49 A warn   B dawn   C scorn   D barn

50 A wise   B cries   C rice   D sighs

Test 350 D

Choose the correct answer. Only one answer is correct.

We arrived . .1. . Spain for the first time . .2. . and I decided to buy a car because we had sold . .3. . we had in England before leaving. Yesterday the sales office rang us . .4. . the car was ready. I had tried out a model . .5. . it before but as I was . .6. . in this city, my wife did not . .7. . it on my own so we went together to . .8. . . We paid . .9. . and signed the papers. They told us that . .10. . us to a garage, . .11. . we could fill up. The . .12. . the office was . .13. . and we got there safely. But when I turned into the main road I suddenly saw a lot of cars racing towards me. I got . .14. . . . .15. . by backing into the garage . .16. . and the man behind me shouted at me. "..17. . problem to . .18. . on the right, isn't it?" my wife said. "Yes, if only I . .19. . a few lessons for practice" I replied. "You . .20. . go carefully . .21. . home," my wife said. "You'd be sorry if you had an accident . .22. . the first day, . .23. ." While we were talking, the man behind got out of his car and said in good English "Would you . .24. . me when you are thinking of leaving? Or are you going to sit in your car . .25. . day?"

1 A to
  B in
  C at
  D on

2 A few weeks since
  B since a few weeks
  C few weeks ago
  D a few weeks ago

3 A that
  B which
  C the one
  D the one what

4 A for saying
  B to say
  C for telling
  D to tell

5 A as
  B like
  C the same that
  D similar

6 A no longer used to
    driving
  B still not used to drive
  C not yet used to
    driving
  D already not used to
    drive

7 A want me to collect
  B like me to collect
  C want that I collected
  D like that I collected

8 A bring it
  B take it
  C fetch it
  D carry it away

9 A the car
  B the car for
  C for the car
  D how much the car

10 A there was enough
petrol to take
B there was enough
petrol for taking
C it was enough petrol
to take
D it was enough petrol
for taking

11 A where at
B there
C there where
D where

12 A nearest garage at
B nearest garage to
C garage most near
D most near garage to

13 A at 100 yards away
B at 100 yards far
C about 100 yards away
D about 100 yards far

14 A away from their way
B away from their road
C out of their way
D out their road

15 A as fast as I could
B so fast as I could
C as fast as I may
D so fast as I may

16 A once more
B one more time
C one other time
D another time

17 A It's so much
B It's such a
C That's such a
D That's so much a

18 A remind to drive
B remind driving
C remember to drive
D remember driving

19 A would have
B would have had
C was having
D had had

20 A had better
B would better
C had rather
D would rather

21 A in the way to
B on the way to
C in the way
D on the way

22 A in
B on
C at
D by

23 A hadn't you?
B shouldn't you?
C wouldn't you?
D won't you?

24 A mind to tell
B object telling
C mind telling
D upset to tell

25 A every
B each
C all the
D all

Choose the correct answer. Only one answer is correct.

Waiting for the Guests to Arrive

"I wonder why . .26. . yet. I told Jim how to get here but perhaps I . .27. . a map. The traffic . .28. . them, of course. But I'm sure they would have telephoned us if they . .29. . lost." "Yes, but by the time they . .30. . here, the dinner . .31. . . What a nuisance! I . .32. . to all this trouble. . .33. . getting everything ready."

26 A they didn't arrive
    B didn't they arrive
    C they haven't arrived
    D haven't they arrived

27 A should have given him
    B had to give him
    C ought to give him
    D must have given him

28 A can delay
    B may delay
    C can have delayed
    D may have delayed

29 A would get
    B had got
    C would have got
    D would be got

30 A will get
    B would get
    C get
    D are getting

31 A has been spoilt
    B will be spoilt
    C shall be spoilt
    D is spoilt

32 A needn't have gone
    B didn't need to go
    C mustn't have gone
    D hadn't to go

33 A I am working for hours
    B I have been working for hours
    C It's hours I'm working
    D It's hours I've been working

Choose the correct answer. Only one answer is correct.

34 He was killed in a car . . . . . .
    A blow   B crash   C shock   D hit

35 All the hotels in the town were full up so we stayed in a . . . . . village.
    A close   B neighbour   C near   D nearby

36 He won the first . . . . . in the competition.
    A prize   B price   C reward   D premium

37 Sixty per cent of television viewers chose him as their . . . . . actor.
    A popular   B preferred   C favourite   D favoured

38 We've been . . . . . with that firm for many years.
    A treating   B making business   C dealing   D supplying

39 I can't give you an answer yet. I'd like . . . . . more time to consider my decision.
    A quite   B fairly   C hardly   D rather

40 I learnt to . . . . . a bicycle when I was six years old.
   A drive   B ride   C guide   D conduct

41 The lady who had invited us heard me telling my wife that the dinner was terrible so I
   was . . . . . .
   A confused   B nervous   C shameful   D embarrassed

42 Sometimes a bus . . . . . gets on the bus and checks the tickets.
   A inspector   B agent   C conductor   D officer

43 Where do you . . . . . the writing paper? In this desk?
   A keep   B hold   C maintain   D guard

44 PTO stands . . . . . "Please turn over" – the page, of course.
   A as   B like   C for   D by

45 He'll soon get . . . . . his disappointment and be quite cheerful again by the morning.
   A over   B out of   C away   D through

In this series of questions, three words have the same sound but one does not. Choose the one that does not.

Example: A go   B so   C show   D *do*

46 A case   B phrase   C base   D lace

47 A eight   B height   C weight   D freight

48 A wrong   B young   C sung   D tongue

49 A lower   B shower   C tower   D power

50 A sound   B ground   C drowned   D owned

Test 400 A

Choose the correct answer. Only one answer is correct.

One crossing of the Atlantic is very much like . .1. . ; and people who cross it frequently do not . .2. . for the . .3. . of its interest. Most of us are quite happy when we feel . .4. . to go to bed and pleased when the journey . .5. . . On the first night this time I felt especially lazy and went to bed . .6. . earlier than usual. When I . .7. . my cabin, I was surprised . .8. . that I . .9. . a companion during my trip. I had expected . .10. . but there was a suitcase . .11. . mine in the opposite corner. I wondered who . .12. . . Soon afterwards he came in. He was the sort of man you might meet . .13. . , except that he was wearing . .14. . good clothes that I made up my mind that we would not . .15. . , . .16. . , and did not say . .17. . .

I suppose I slept for several hours because when I woke up it was the middle of the night. I felt cold but covered . .18. . . .19. . and tried to . .20. . . Then I realised that a draught was coming from somewhere. I got up . .21. . the door but found it already locked from the inside. The cold air was coming from the window opposite. I crossed the room and . .22. . the moon shone through it on to the other bed. . .23. . there. It took me a minute or two to . .24. . the door myself. I realised that my companion . .25. . through the window into the sea.

1 A other
  B the other
  C another
  D one other

2 A make the travel
  B make the voyage
  C do the travel
  D do the voyage

3 A reason
  B motive
  C cause
  D sake

4 A tired enough
  B enough tired
  C ourselves tired enough
  D ourselves enough tired

5 A is achieved
  B finish
  C is over
  D is in the end

6 A quite
  B rather
  C fairly
  D somehow

7 A arrived in
  B reached to
  C arrived to
  D reached at

8 A for seeing
  B that I saw
  C at seeing
  D to see

9 A would have had
  B should have had
  C was to have
  D ought to have

10 A being lonely
   B to be lonely
   C being alone
   D to be alone

11 A like
   B as
   C similar than
   D the same that

12 A could he be and how
       he would be
    B he could be and what
       he would be like
    C could he be and what
       would he be like
    D he could be and he
       would be

13 A in each place
    B for all parts
    C somewhere
    D anywhere

14 A a so
    B so
    C such a
    D such

15 A treat together well
    B pass together well
    C get on well together
    D go by well together

16 A whoever he was
    B whoever was he
    C however he was
    D however was he

17 A him a single word
    B him not one word
    C a single word to him
    D not one word to him

18 A up me
    B up myself
    C up to myself
    D myself up

19 A so well as I could
    B as well as I could
    C so well that I might
    D as well that I might

20 A go back to sleep
    B go back to sleeping
    C put myself to sleep
       again
    D put myself for
       sleeping again

21 A to shut
    B for shutting
    C in order that I shut
    D so as for shutting

22 A while doing like that
    B as I did like that
    C as I did so
    D at doing so

23 A It was no one
    B There was no one
    C It was anyone
    D There was anyone

24 A remind to lock
    B remember to lock
    C remind locking
    D remember locking

25 A had to jump
    B was to have jumped
    C must have jumped
    D could be jumped

Choose the correct answer. Only one answer is correct.

In a Restaurant

"..26.. I ask the waiter for the bill, darling, when you ..27.. your coffee?"

"Yes, I think you ..28... I ..29.. this film for such a long time that I ..30.. any of it."

"Waiter! The bill, please. Oh dear, I haven't got my wallet. I ..31.. it in my other jacket. I wish I ..32.. it before we came out."

"Good heavens! Now I suppose they'll make us ..33.."

26 A Shall
   B Will
   C Am I going
   D Ought

27 A will finish
   B shall finish
   C will have finished
   D have finished

28 A had rather
   B would rather
   C had better
   D would better

29 A am looking forward
     to seeing
   B am looking forward
     to see
   C have been looking
     forward to seeing
   D have been looking
     forward to see

30 A wouldn't like that we
     miss
   B wouldn't like to miss
   C wouldn't miss
   D wouldn't like that we
     missed

31 A must have left
   B had to leave
   C should have left
   D ought to leave

32 A would check
   B have checked
   C would have checked
   D had checked

33 A to wash up
   B wash up
   C washing up
   D the washing up

Choose the correct answer. Only one answer is correct.

34 He . . . . . out of the window for a moment and then went on working.
   A glanced   B viewed   C glimpsed   D regarded

35 It's the . . . . . in this country to go out and pick flowers on the first day of spring.
   A use   B custom   C habit   D normal

36 He made a swift . . . . . from his illness.
   A repair   B survival   C relief   D recovery

37 It gave me a strange feeling of excitement to see my name in . . . . . .
   A news   B print   C publication   D press

38 You'd better add it up. I'm no good at . . . . . .
   A counters   B characters   C summaries   D figures

39 Our main concern is to raise the voters' . . . . . of living.
   A standard   B capacity   C degree   D conditions

40 I'd like to take . . . . . of this opportunity to thank you all for your co-operation.
  A profit   B benefit   C advantage   D occasion

41 He . . . . . to hit me if I didn't do as he said.
  A pretended   B thought   C threatened   D warned

42 He doesn't feel like playing tennis because he's . . . . . .
  A out of condition   B off condition
  C off fitness   D out of fitness

43 He's been working too hard and he's . . . . . . He needs a rest.
  A broken apart   B broken up   C run down   D run over

44 We went to the station to . . . . . .
  A see them out   B see them off   C goodbye them   D say them goodbye

45 New problems are always . . . . . in the factory.
  A raising   B going up   C waking up   D coming up

In this series of questions, three words have the same sound but one does not. Choose the one that does not.

Example: A go   B so   C show   D *do*

46 A spear   B wear   C dare   D prayer

47 A spread   B tread   C bread   D bead

48 A blow   B allow   C owe   D sew

49 A dose   B prose   C flows   D knows

50 A crime   B limb   C climb   D rhyme

Test 400 B

Choose the correct answer. Only one answer is correct.

"I can't understand . .1. . ," Mark said. "The couple had lived in this house for a long time. Their relatives lived next door to them and in another . .2. . . Hadley, the . .3. . , called in to see them five minutes after the postman delivered a letter. But they had already disappeared."

The house . .4. . had . .5. . surprises for Mr Bolton. It was exactly as he had imagined it. . .6. . in the hall and front room, but the kitchen and dining room were clearly used . .7. . and possessed . .8. . . Someone without much money, but . .9. . nice things, had lived there. He or she – and he thought it was probably she – had been generous, too, . .10. . her efforts to save, if the packets of little things obviously bought at the door were anything to go by. The thin detective . .11. . wandered through the house. There was no sign of flight, packing, . .12. . violence. He looked at everything but . .13. . seemed to interest him was a photograph . .14. . when the couple had got married. It was an ordinary picture but he . .15. . it. Nora looked rather frightened, and Alex, the husband, although he seemed determined, had a worried expression. . .16. . smiled confidently.

"I don't think Hadley is the sort of man who imagines things," Mark said. "When he says he felt the couple had been in the house that morning, . .17. . , I believe him. But here's another photograph of Alex. He . .18. . someone I knew in the army, . .19. . in normal circumstances but . .20. . quickly if necessary." "They seem . .21. . just after the postman called," Bolton said. "I wonder if they won the football pools and the news of their win . .22. . in the letter. They may have gone away quickly in case . .23. . . Perhaps Alex knew his wife was generous and . .24. . a decision . .25. . the money with her relatives."

1 A that which happened
  B that which did happen
  C what did happen
  D what happened

2 A house nearby
  B near house
  C facing house
  D house in the way

3 A wife brother
  B brother wife
  C wife's brother
  D brother's wife

4 A by its own
  B as itself
  C for itself
  D itself

5 A little
  B a little
  C few
  D a few

6 A It wasn't much
    furniture
  B There wasn't much
    furniture
  C They weren't many
    furnitures
  D There weren't many
    furnitures

7 A a great deal
  B a big lot
  C much
  D the most of the time

8 A its proper character
  B a character of its own
  C their proper character
  D a character of their own

9 A which liked
  B who liked
  C what liked
  D to whom liked

10 A in spite of
   B although
   C nevertheless
   D however

11 A with the glasses of horn rims
   B in the glasses of horn rims
   C with the horn-rimmed glasses
   D of the horn-rimmed glasses

12 A or
   B nor
   C but
   D neither

13 A the only thing that
   B the only thing what
   C the single thing what
   D the only which

14 A done
   B made
   C caught
   D taken

15 A did a careful study of
   B made a careful study of
   C did a careful study from
   D made a careful study from

16 A The whole of the relatives
   B All relatives
   C The relatives all
   D The relatives they all

17 A as happy as never
   B as happy as ever
   C so happy as never
   D so happy as ever

18 A remembers me of
   B reminds me of
   C remembers me to
   D reminds me to

19 A enough calm
   B so calmly
   C calm enough
   D just calmly

20 A able for acting
   B was able to act
   C capable to act
   D capable of acting

21 A to leave
   B to be leaving
   C to have left
   D that they left

22 A was
   B were
   C it was
   D they were

23 A the rest of the family found out
   B the rest of the family would find out
   C the others of the family found out
   D the others of the family would find out

24 A should do
   B should make
   C had to do
   D had to make

25 A for not sharing
   B in order to not share
   C so as not to share
   D not to be shared

Choose the correct answer. Only one answer is correct.

On the Main Road

"Slow down, darling. You're driving much too fast."

"I know. But by the time we ..26.. to the church, the marriage service ..27.. started. If you ..28.. such a long time to get dressed, we'd have been there by now. I finished ..29.. an hour before you did."

"It's not my fault. You ..30.. we were in a hurry."

"Now there's a police car behind us. It's signalling. I ..31.. stop."

"Would you ..32.. me your driving licence, sir? You realise that you were driving at a hundred miles an hour, don't you?"

"No, officer, I ..33.. Oh, well, I suppose I was. We're going to a wedding, you see."

"Not now, sir, I'm afraid. You're coming to the police station."

26 A shall get
    B shall arrive
    C get
    D arrive

27 A shall have
    B will have
    C has
    D must have

28 A hadn't taken
    B wouldn't have taken
    C weren't taking
    D wouldn't take

29 A dressing
    B to dress
    C being dressed
    D my dressing

30 A must have told me
    B ought to tell me
    C had to tell me
    D should have told me

31 A had rather
    B would rather
    C had better
    D would better

32 A mind to show
    B mind showing
    C matter to show
    D matter showing

33 A didn't need to be
    B may not have been
    C couldn't have been
    D needn't have been

Choose the correct answer. Only one answer is correct.

34 He . . . . . the letter carefully before putting it in the envelope.
    A folded   B bent   C turned   D curved

35 I . . . . . you to go to the Town Hall and ask them for information about it.
    A advertise   B announce   C notice   D advise

36 He wasn't admitted to the club because he wasn't a . . . . . .
    A partner   B member   C social   D representative

37 You must . . . . . facts and not run away from the truth.
    A look   B sight   C front   D face

38 I . . . . . to him for the error.
    A excused   B apologised   C pardoned   D forgave

39 She's bought some lovely . . . . . to make herself a dress.
  A material   B clothing   C costume   D pattern

40 He's staying in the youth . . . . . in Market Street.
  A home   B lodge   C hostel   D house

41 It's no use ringing me at the office this week because I'm . . . . . .
  A by my leave   B at leave   C in holidays   D on holiday

42 . . . . . at the Town Hall, the Queen was welcomed by the Mayor.
  A On reaching   B At arrival   C On arrival   D At reaching

43 He . . . . . working till he was seventy years old.
  A kept on   B kept up   C followed   D succeeded

44 The meeting . . . . . at midnight and we all went home.
  A broke through   B stopped off   C stopped up   D broke up

45 He's not as honest as he . . . . . .
  A makes up   B makes out   C gives over   D gives away

In this series of questions, three words have the same sound but one does not. Choose the one that does not.

Example: A go   B so   D show   D *do*

46 A drum   B thumb   C home   D come

47 A abroad   B load   C scored   D board

48 A bush   B brush   C crush   D rush

49 A worm   B storm   C form   D norm

50 A cast   B classed   C passed   D massed

Test 400 C

Choose the correct answer. Only one answer is correct.

The news did not come directly to Ella herself. . .1. . her indirectly in hints that she had won the prize. But as she was a calm, quiet girl, she . .2. . without . .3. . , . .4. . the whole school was full of rumours and statements from students who had no right to be . .5. . at all because . .6. . really knew . .7. . what the result of this year's art competition was.

But Ella was . .8. . good artist, her lines so sure, that . .9. . student in the art class was expected to win. But you never . .10. . Last year nobody had expected Frank Peters to win with that funny modern painting he had . .11. . the city bridge. .12. . , it was hard to . .13. . the bridge until you looked at the picture for a long time. Still, Frank had got the prize and the President of the Board of Governors had presented . .14. . at a big dinner in the Ritz Hotel.

Ella was a rather shy girl but her classmates seldom thought of her . .15. . shy. She was pretty and intelligent and . .16. . very well with everyone. She played games well, had taken part in the school play, and never seemed to . .17. . , except in pleasant ways. She liked her school. She was very fond of her art teacher, Miss Drake, . .18. . was natural. .19. . wonderful about Miss Drake was that she brought out the best in her students – not . .20. . but theirs. . .21. . best, . .22. . , was not good enough to please Miss Drake. So Ella was . .23. . the prize, not just for herself and her parents but because she had heard Miss Drake . .24. . that it was the . .25. . seen from one of her students.

1 A It reached
   B They reached
   C It arrived at
   D They arrived at

2 A went on to work
   B went on working
   C went back for work
   D went back working

3 A telling nothing
   B telling anything
   C saying nothing
   D saying anything

4 A in spite
   B nevertheless
   C although
   D however

5 A doing advertisements
   B making advertise-
      ments
   C doing announcements
   D making announce-
      ments

6 A no one
   B some one
   C anyone
   D not anyone

7 A still
   B already
   C yet
   D any longer

8 A such a
   B such
   C a so
   D so

9 A not another
   B no one other
   C no other
   D none other

10 A might know
    B could be sure
    C can learn
    D may be secure

11 A done for
    B made about
    C done of
    D made on

12 A In the reality
    B To say truth
    C Surely
    D In fact

13 A pick up
    B see through
    C take hold of
    D make out

14 A him it
    B it to him
    C it him
    D him for it

15 A as
    B like
    C to be
    D for

16 A got on
    B got by
    C passed
    D carried

17 A distinguish
    B stand off
    C stand out
    D stand up

18 A which
    B what
    C that
    D whose

19 A The thing what was
    B What was
    C The
    D The which was

20 A her best herself
    B her best self
    C her own best
    D her proper best

21 A Other person's
    B Other peoples'
    C Anybody's else
    D Anybody else's

22 A for how good it might
      be
    B for how good might
      it be
    C however good it was
    D however good was it

23 A looking forward to
      win
    B looking forward to
      winning
    C wishing to win
    D waiting for winning

24 A say
    B tell
    C to say
    D to tell

25 A better painting she
      ever had
    B best painting she ever
      had
    C better painting she
      had ever
    D best painting she had
      ever

Choose the correct answer. Only one answer is correct.

At the Tourist Information Office

"I have been looking for this office since I arrived at the station. It ..26.. be in the main street. I ..27.. me a hotel, please."

"Certainly, sir. But you ..28.. so far. If you'd turned left at the station, you ..29.. it straightaway. Now, ..30.. see if we can find you something suitable?"

"I only want a room for one night but I can't stand sleeping in noisy rooms."

"All the hotels here are near the main road. You ..31.. come home with me, sir. You'll be more comfortable. In fact, when you ..32.. my wife's cooking, you'll realise you ..33.. have come to a better place."

26 A should
   B has to
   C ought
   D must

27 A would like you finding
   B would like you to find
   C would like that you find
   D am wanting you to find

28 A didn't need to walk
   B needn't have walked
   C mustn't have walked
   D weren't to walk

29 A would have found
   B had found
   C should have found
   D would find

30 A let's to
   B are we going to
   C will we
   D shall we

31 A had better
   B would better
   C had rather
   D would rather

32 A will be tasting
   B shall taste
   C taste
   D will taste

33 A can't
   B might not
   C may not
   D couldn't

Choose the correct answer. Only one answer is correct.

34 She chose some very pretty . . . . . paper for the present.
   A covering   B involving   C packing   D wrapping

35 Everyone else was killed in the accident. I was the only one to . . . . . .
   A relieve   B survive   C alive   D outlive

36 That's a nice dress. It . . . . . you perfectly.
   A suits   B costumes   C matches   D goes

37 The . . . . . stuck on the outside of the envelope said "By Air".
   A label   B ticket   C signal   D advertisement

38 She died after a long . . . . . .
   A disease   B sickness   C illness   D failing

39 I . . . . . to inform you that there's nothing we can do to help you.

    A sorry   B respect   C resent   D regret

40 I'll put the flowers in this . . . . . . They'll look nice there.

    A mug   B vase   C crystal   D bucket

41 . . . : . I didn't understand the job but now I'm making progress.

    A On the beginning   B At first

    C For a start   D In principle

42 Would you mind paying for the tickets . . . . . ?

    A in advance   B forwards   C primarily   D now and then

43 How long did it take you to realise he was dishonest? I . . . . . from the start.

    A looked him through   B saw through him

    C looked forward to him   D saw him through

44 We're going to have our house . . . . . . The decorators are coming next week.

    A done up   B done in   C made over   D made away with

45 He asked me what was . . . . . in the street outside.

    A succeeding   B making out   C doing up   D going on

In this series of questions, three words have the same sound but one does not. Choose the one that does not.

Example: A go   B so   C show   D *do*

46 A freeze   B ease   C seize   D lease

47 A weight   B great   C wheat   D freight

48 A palm   B calm   C warm   D harm

49 A hint   B mint   C print   D pint

50 A stuff   B cough   C rough   D enough

Test 400 D

Choose the correct answer. Only one answer is correct.

As you probably know, our host . .1. ., Duncairn is one of a small group of castles built . .2. . the twelfth century on the western coast of Scotland. Only one of its sea-walls still stands. It is . .3. . a few feet high, . .4. . an entrance gate with . .5. . of a stone stairway that originally rose up to the wall walk. I had a theory that it was the work of a particular architect who had built some other castles on the coast. . .6. . I had decided to . .7. . Duncairn to see if it would confirm my theory.

I was . .8. . a farmer living . .9. . . .10. . the castle, who was quite pleased to put me up. He seemed interested in my work and used to join me every evening . .11. . together from the castle. On the night before I . .12. ., I told him I wanted to go back to the castle to check a detail I was not sure of.

"You'd never . .13. . there by night, . .14. . you?" he said.

"Of course. I won't be long."

"You can't go there after dark," he replied. "You would never come back. The wall would shut you in. Didn't you ever wonder why . .15. . with you every night? It was to make sure that you would not be shut in, . .16. . the rest of them."

I thought he had gone a little mad, . .17. . sometimes happens to people who . .18. . . Then he told me a strange story about a war between two families that had ended in . .19. . brutal way that one of them had killed the others and put them in the wall, believing that it would help to hold it up. "I cannot let you go back there," the farmer said, "in case you are . .20. . ."

"I . .21. . don't see that . .22. . danger," I said, laughing. ". .23. . the ghosts are holding up the wall, it won't fall on me."

". .24. . has ever gone there at night and come back alive," he said. "The ghosts are . .25. . tired and need others to help them."

1 A was explaining to us
  B was explaining us
  C was remarking us
  D was telling to us
	4 A in spite there is yet
	  B in spite it is still
	  C though it is yet
	  D though there is still

2 A by
  B at
  C in
  D on
	5 A what stays
	  B what remains
	  C that what remains
	  D that what stays

3 A hardly more than
  B almost more than
  C just as much as
  D nearly more than
	6 A Because of that
	  B For that
	  C That is the cause why
	  D For which reason

7 A do a careful study to
B make a careful study to
C do a careful study of
D make a careful study
of

8 A enough lucky to find
B lucky enough to find
C with enough luck to
meet
D with luck enough to
meet

9 A by his own
B without no one
C by himself
D solely

10 A quite near at
B not much far from
C nearby to
D not far away from

11 A so that we could walk
home
B so that we could walk
to home
C for walking home
D for walking to home

12 A was to leave
B would be to leave
C must have left
D must be left

13 A pretend to go
B pretend going
C think of going
D think to go

14 A should
B did
C would
D had

15 A have I always come
back
B I have always come
back
C have I come back
always
D I have come back
always

16 A similar than
B the same that
C as
D like

17 A what
B which
C that
D for

18 A do live alone
B do live lonely
C live alone
D live lonely

19 A a so
B what a
C the most
D such a

20 A avoided to leave
B prevented to leave
C avoided from leaving
D prevented from
leaving

21 A still
B yet
C already
D no longer

22 A it is any
B it is some
C there is any
D there is some

23 A Meanwhile
B During
C As long as
D As far as

24 A None
B No one
C Anyone
D Not one

25 A getting
B getting to be
C becoming that they
are
D becoming to be

Choose the correct answer. Only one answer is correct.

After a Road Accident

"Now, sir, you saw the accident, I believe. Would you mind . .26. . me what happened?"

"Not at all, constable. The driver of the red car was parked there. He . .27. . when a black Mini came up very quickly. If he . .28. . in his mirror he would have seen the Mini coming. But he . .29. . in a hurry. The Mini hit him but didn't stop."

"Did you take down the Mini's number?"

"No. Now I wish I . .30. . . I've never seen a driver before who didn't stop after an accident."

"The Mini . .31. ., sir. That . .32. . explain it. I'll take down your name and address in case you . .33. . as a witness."

26 A to tell
   B telling
   C to say
   D saying

27 A was just moving out
   B has just moved out
   C would just move out
   D is just moving out

28 A would look
   B did look
   C would have looked
   D had looked

29 A ought to be
   B should have been
   C had to be
   D must have been

30 A would have
   B did
   C had
   D would

31 A may have been stolen
   B can have been stolen
   C may have been robbed
   D can have been robbed

32 A ought
   B has to
   C would
   D did

33 A will be needed
   B are needed
   C will need
   D need

Choose the correct answer. Only one answer is correct.

34 He . . . . . his head, wondering how to solve the problem.
   A screwed   B scraped   C wound   D scratched

35 I . . . . . him some money and must pay him back tomorrow.
   A debt   B borrow   C owe   D own

36 Steak pie! That's my favourite . . . . . .
   A menu   B receipt   C dish   D plate

37 His shoes were so old that his . . . . . were sticking out of them.
   A toes   B tips   C thumbs   D fingers

38 He was . . . . . from the firm because he was always late for work.
   A sacked   B retired   C resigned   D disposed

39 She got married although her parents had not given her their . . . . . .
   A allowance   B consent   C permit   D let

40 The flight was supposed to take off at eight o'clock but . . . . . we had to wait until nine.
   A in effect   B for an end   C on purpose   D for result

41 I agree with him . . . . . , but not entirely.
   A until a certain point   B to some point
   C to some extent   D until a certain extent

42 Everything I've described went wrong. . . . . . , the whole affair was a disaster.
   A In small   B In short   C Summarily   D In brief words

43 Did you . . . . . the examination last year?
   A take place in   B enter into   C go in for   D form part of

44 We were . . . . . for half an hour in the traffic and so we arrived late.
   A put back   B broken down   C held up   D kept off

45 The dog was . . . . . by a bus and killed.
   A run over   B tripped up   C knocked out   D fallen down

In this series of questions, three words have the same sound but one does not. Choose the one that does not.

Example: A go   B so   C show   D *do*

46 A haste   B waste   C raced   D praised

47 A part   B quart   C start   D heart

48 A ever   B sever   C fever   D clever

49 A speak   B break   C beak   D seek

50 A juice   B goose   C choose   D loose

Test 450 A

Choose the correct answer. Only one answer is correct.

It . .1. . around nine o'clock when I drove . .2. . home from work because it was already dark. As I approached the gates I switched off the headlamps of the car . .3. . prevent the beam from swinging in through the window and waking Jack, who shared the house with me. But I . .4. . . I noticed that his light was still on, so he was awake anyway – unless he'd . .5. . asleep while reading. I put the car away and went up the steps. Then I opened the door quietly and went to Jack's room. He was in bed awake but he didn't . .6. . turn towards me.

"What's up, Jack?" I said.

"For God's . .7. . don't make a noise," he said.

The way he spoke reminded me . .8. . someone . .9. . who is afraid to talk in case he . .10. . himself a serious injury.

"Take your shoes . .11. ., Neville," Jack said.

I thought that he must be ill and that . .12. . humour him to keep him happy. "There's a snake here," he explained. " It's asleep . .13. . the sheets. I was . .14. . on my back reading when I saw it. I knew that moving was out of . .15. . . I . .16. . moved even if I'd wanted to." I realised that he was . .17. . . "I was relying . .18. . you to call a doctor as soon as you . .19. . home," Jack went on. "It hasn't bitten me yet but I daren't . .20. . to upset it. It . .21. . wake up. I'm sick . .22. . this," he said. "I . .23. . that you'd be home an hour ago."

There was no time to argue or apologise . .24. . late. I looked at him . .25. . I could and went out to telephone the doctor.

1 A had to be
  B was to be
  C must have been
  D should have been

2 A at
  B back
  C in
  D to

3 A so as to
  B in order
  C so that
  D for

4 A needn't bother
  B didn't need to bother
  C needn't have bothered
  D mustn't have bothered

5 A become
  B fallen
  C gone
  D grown

6 A even
  B just
  C only
  D rather

7 A behalf
  B love
  C reason
  D sake

8 A from
  B to
  C of
  D with

9 A with pain
   B in pain
   C having pain
   D having ache

10 A would do
   B does
   C would make
   D makes

11 A off
   B out
   C away
   D back

12 A I had rather
   B I would rather
   C I had better
   D I would better

13 A between
   B beside
   C below
   D behind

14 A lied
   B laid
   C laying
   D lying

15 A the bargain
   B the question
   C the chance
   D the risk

16 A may not have
   B might not have
   C can't have
   D couldn't have

17 A in fact
   B in serious
   C in earnest
   D in truth

18 A on
   B to
   C in
   D for

19 A would come
   B have come
   C were coming
   D came

20 A to do a thing
   B do anything
   C to do something
   D do nothing

21 A might
   B can
   C should
   D shall

22 A with
   B from
   C of
   D for

23 A made it certain
   B have been assured
   C counted on
   D took it for granted

24 A for being
   B to be
   C on being
   D to have been

25 A as fiercely as
   B as encouragingly as
   C so bravely as
   D so hopefully as

Choose the correct answer. Only one answer is correct.

26 The bank is offering a . . . . . to anyone who can give information about the robbery.
  A compensation   B prize   C reward   D premium

27 Don't leave your bicycle out in the rain. It'll get . . . . . .
  A rusty   B crude   C rough   D tough

28 The landlord told him to leave because he hadn't paid his . . . . . .
  A due   B fee   C hire   D rent

29 She's fainted. Throw some water on her face and she may . . . . . .
  A come round   B come back   C come again   D come out

30 I'm afraid you've been . . . . . . This bank note is a forgery.
  A taken in   B taken up   C taken down   D taken out

31 They're . . . . . to build a big factory on the site.
  A planning   B thinking   C projecting   D pretending

32 I couldn't . . . . . the meeting because I was so busy.
  A assist   B attend   C attempt   D present

33 We've . . . . . sugar. Ask Mrs Jones to lend us some.
  A run away with   B run down   C run off   D run out of

34 He has been . . . . . of murdering his wife.
  A blamed   B charged   C accused   D arrested

35 Drive carefully because there are a lot of . . . . . in the road for the next few miles.
  A curls   B folds   C crosses   D bends

36 The printing of the book has been held up by the paper . . . . . .
  A scarce   B shortage   C lack   D deficit

37 I . . . . . you that the goods will be delivered next week.
  A confirm   B assure   C undertake   D insist

38 In many . . . . . factories, machines often do work previously done by men.
  A actual   B nowadays   C novel   D modern

39 The second World War . . . . . in 1939.
  A broke out   B broke off   C broke up   D broke open

40 A foreign firm have bought the shares in his company and . . . . . .
  A got over it   B taken it over   C overtaken it   D overcome it

For each of the following phrases, four suggested explanations of the meaning are given, only one of which is correct. Choose the correct one.

41 That would be far better
  A It would be a great improvement
  B It's not right here
  C It would work better at long distance
  D The further away it is, the better

42 You ought to stand up to him
  A You should get up when he comes in
  B You should support him
  C You shouldn't be afraid to argue with him
  D You are probably about the same height as he is

43 He asked me out
  A He wanted me to go outside
  B He told me he would meet me outside
  C He had some questions for me when I got outside
  D He invited me to go out with him

44 Never mind
  A It doesn't bear thinking about
  B Don't be upset about it
  C It's none of your business
  D You needn't remember it

45 They'll be sent to you in due course
  A You'll get them in the correct order
  B They'll arrive at the right time
  C You'll receive them after the normal space of time has passed
  D They'll be given to you when you've paid for your studies

In each case, there is one word with the same sound as the word given in capital letters but with different spelling. Choose which one of the four definitions given defines this word correctly.

Example: STALK
  A fixed
  B *a bird* (stork)
  C compartment for an animal
  D supply in store

46 WAIT
  A grain for making bread
  B the colour of snow
  C how heavy a thing is
  D opposite of dry

47 HEARD
  A opposite of soft
  B injured
  C store of money
  D number of animals

48 FLOWER
  A surface of a room
  B powder made from grain
  C bright flame
  D river

49 MAIL
  A breakfast, lunch etc
  B masculine
  C machine for grinding
  D measure of distance in Britain

50 SIDE
  A place where something is being built
  B ability to see
  C breathed out in relief
  D place to sit down

Test 450 B

Choose the correct answer. Only one answer is correct.

She . .1. . asleep where she . .2. ., without undressing. Her first thought when she woke up was that it had started raining again. She waited for the sound that had woken her . .3. .. It came again . .4. . a moment, a shower of earth thrown against the window . .5. . from the yard outside.

She realised that she might be . .6. . danger. Someone with . .7. . idea of the geography of the inn . .8. . mistaken her window . .9. . the landlord's. But curiosity got the better of her caution in the end. She . .10. . towards the window . .11. . and hid in the shadow of the wall.

She had not been mistaken, . .12. .. There was a man standing beneath her window. He . .13. . again to the ground and then aimed another piece of earth . .14. . her window. This time she recognised his face and the shock made her . .15. . in surprise, forgetting the caution . .16. . she . .17. .. It was John. She . .18. . forward . .19. ., opening her window, and . .20. . to him if he had not . .21. . his hand . .22. . silence. Then he cupped his hand round his mouth and . .23. ., "Come down and let me in."

She . .24. . her head. "I can't", she said. "I've been locked in." He looked up at the house as if he . .25. . how to climb up and rescue her.

1 A had gone
  B had become
  C had grown
  D had fallen

2 A laid
  B was laying
  C was lying
  D had laid

3 A to reproduce
  B to be repeated
  C to be recurred
  D to repeat

4 A at
  B in
  C on
  D during

5 A pane
  B glass
  C crystal
  D sheet

6 A under
  B on
  C with
  D in

7 A any
  B some
  C no
  D few

8 A should have
  B may have
  C might have
  D can have

9 A with
  B for
  C by
  D to

10 A crept
   B rushed
   C stumbled
   D sprang

11 A so quietly as she might
   B so quietly as she could
   C as quietly as she might
   D as quietly as she could

12 A although
   B despite
   C yet
   D though

13 A inclined
   B leant
   C bent
   D fell

14 A to
   B at
   C on
   D in

15 A to excite
   B excite
   C to exclaim
   D exclaim

16 A to which
   B with which
   C which
   D what

17 A had educated
   B had brought up
   C had trained herself
   D had practised herself

18 A leant
   B approached
   C glanced
   D glimpsed

19 A at first
   B at best
   C at least
   D at once

20 A would call
   B would have called
   C had called
   D should have called

21 A raised
   B risen
   C got up
   D rose

22 A with
   B at
   C in
   D on

23 A whispered
   B told
   C screamed
   D spoke

24 A nodded
   B shook
   C waved
   D dropped

25 A was wondering
   B would wonder
   C was wandering
   D would wander

Choose the correct answer. Only one answer is correct.

26 I enjoyed that dish very much. Would you mind letting me have the . . . . . for it?
   A menu   B prescription   C receipt   D recipe

27 In the days before typewriters were invented, thousands of people were employed as
   . . . . . , copying down figures by hand.
   A dependants   B clerks   C assistants   D officials

28 She . . . . . and fell from the top of the stairs to the bottom.
   A slipped   B sloped   C split   D spilt

29 The professor thanked the audience for listening to his . . . . . on Shakespeare.

    A lecture   B conference   C rehearsal   D recital

30 No one imagined that the apparently . . . . . business man was really a criminal.

    A respectful   B respective   C respectable   D reverent

31 There was an interesting . . . . . of the film in the paper this morning.

    A comment   B résumé   C revision   D review

32 He bought his house on the . . . . . plan, paying a certain amount of money each month.

    A piece   B share   C instalment   D part

33 The good service at the hotel . . . . . the poor food to some extent.

    A made up for   B made up   C made for   D made out

34 We can never relax in this office. New problems are continually . . . . . .

    A coming out   B coming up   C raising   D presenting

35 I didn't realise you wanted to keep the letter. I've . . . . . it up.

    A broken   B pulled   C smashed   D torn

36 His parents died in a motor accident when he was young so he was brought up by a . . . . . .

    A warden   B stepfather   C father-in-law   D guardian

37 I sometimes have . . . . . to visit Birmingham on business.

    A opportunity   B possibility   C occasion   D chance

38 If you . . . . . in taking this attitude, we'll have to ask you to leave.

    A persist   B insist   C resist   D pursue

39 He talked so much during the match that he . . . . . my game.

    A put me out of   B put me off   C put me away from   D put me apart from

40 He . . . . . his engagement just before the wedding.

    A broke out of   B broke away from   C broke off   D broke up

For each of the following phrases, four suggested explanations of the meaning are given, only one of which is correct. Choose the correct one.

41 He calls in from time to time
   A He often comes to see us
   B He visits us occasionally
   C He visits us every hour
   D He sometimes comes to stay for a while

42 What's up?
   A What's the matter?
   B What's the news?
   C What's needed?
   D What's improved?

43 It's as broad as it's long as far as I'm concerned
   A I want a clear answer, one way or the other
   B It makes no difference to me, either way
   C It doesn't make sense to me
   D I think it's a square

44 That child is always up to something
   A He is naughty
   B He likes climbing
   C He likes making things
   D He's never left behind

45 You'll be all right in the long run
   A You'll all be on the same side when it comes to the point
   B All of you will prove to be correct eventually
   C In the end you'll have no need to worry
   D You'll do well in the long-distance race

In each case, there is one word with the same sound as the word given in capital letters but with different spelling. Choose which one of the four definitions given defines this word correctly.

Example: STALK
   A fixed
   B *a bird* (stork)
   C compartment for an animal
   D supply in store

46 CAUGHT
   A something worn
   B child's bed
   C vehicle pulled by a horse
   D place where law cases are heard

47 STAIR
   A look at fixedly
   B direct the course of a ship
   C move (soup, etc.)
   D bright light in the sky

48 NONE
   A famous
   B part of speech
   C woman belonging to a religious order
   D midday

49 PAIN
   A tree
   B sheet of glass
   C handing over money
   D used to fasten papers

50 SEEN
   A action against God's laws
   B opposite of mad
   C write one's name on a document
   D part of a play in the theatre

Test 450 C

Choose the correct answer. Only one answer is correct.

Having passed what I considered the worst obstacle, our spirits . .1 . . . We made towards the left of the cliff, where the going was better, though . .2 . . steeper. Here we found . .3 . . snow, as most of it seemed . .4 . . blown off the mountain. There was no . .5 . . of the mountains in the distance because clouds were forming all round us.

About 1 o'clock a storm came up suddenly. We . .6 . . its approach but we were concentrating on cutting steps, and before we had time . .7 . . anything, we were . .8 . . by snow. We could not move up or down and had to wait motionless, getting . .9 . . . . .10 . . my hood, my nose and cheeks were frostbitten and I . .11 . . a hand out of my glove to warm them.

After two hours of this, I realised we would have to do something to avoid . .12 . . death where we stood. . .13 . . through the mist I had . .14 . . the . .15 . . of a dark buttress just above us; to descend in this wind was . .16 . . ; our only hope was to . .17 . . up to this buttress, and dig out a platform at the foot of it . .18 . . we could pitch our tent.

We climbed to this place and started to cut away the ice. . .19 . . my companion seemed to regard the situation . .20 . . hopeless but . .21 . . the wind died away and he cheered up. At last we had made a platform . .22 . . the tent, and we did this . .23 . . . We . .24 . . into our sleeping bags and . .25 . . asleep, feeling that we were lucky to be still alive.

1 A rose
  B raised
  C arose
  D aroused

2 A quite
  B fairly
  C rather
  D hardly

3 A few
  B a few
  C little
  D a little

4 A that it had
  B to have been
  C it was
  D to be

5 A view
  B vision
  C spectacle
  D outlook

6 A may not have noticed
  B had to notice
  C must have noticed
  D ought to have noticed

7 A to make
  B for making
  C to do
  D for doing

8 A blinded
  B deafened
  C unsighted
  D unseen

9 A more cold and more
    cold
  B colder and colder
  C more frozen and more
    frozen
  D frozen and frozen

10 A In spite of
    B Instead of
    C In case of
    D Although

11 A dared not to bring
    B dared not bring
    C dared not to take
    D dared not take

12 A to be frozen in
    B to be frozen to
    C being frozen in
    D being frozen to

13 A Every time
    B At the time
    C From time to time
    D For the time being

14 A made out
    B seen through
    C glimpsed to
    D remarked

15 A outcome
    B overcome
    C outline
    D shade

16 A off the point
    B out of the question
    C beyond the reach
    D out of touch

17 A slide
    B slip
    C stagger
    D scramble

18 A in which
    B on which
    C in that
    D on that

19 A At first
    B At principle
    C At once
    D On the beginning

20 A for
    B to be
    C as
    D like

21 A regularly
    B gradually
    C little to little
    D constantly

22 A enough big to put up
    B big enough to put up
    C enough big for putting up
    D big enough for putting up

23 A the better we can
    B the better we might
    C as best we could
    D as best we may

24 A crawled
    B crushed
    C leapt
    D crashed

25 A went
    B fell
    C became
    D grew

Choose the correct answer. Only one answer is correct.

26 His parents died when he was young so he was . . . . . by his uncle.
   A brought up   B grown up   C brought out   D taken out

27 When he . . . . . at the age of 65, the company will give him a gold watch.
   A dismisses   B resigns   C retires   D pensions

28 The elephant fell into the . . . . . the hunters had set for it.
   A trail   B trap   C trick   D trip

29 The weather forecast was good so it should . . . . . fine after all.
   A turn into   B turn out   C turn over   D turn up

30 I had to stand in a . . . . . for hours to get tickets for the film.
   A file   B tail   C queue   D procession

31 The school claims to be able to . . . . . students English in three months.
   A teach   B explain   C instruct   D learn

32 He'll . . . . . his nervousness once he's on stage.
   A get away   B get off   C get through   D get over

33 As soon as his party came into . . . . . they changed the law.
   A force   B strength   C position   D power

34 Roses are quite . . . . . flowers in English gardens.
   A accustomed   B ordinary   C common   D vulgar

35 You could tell from his big ears that he . . . . . his father.
   A took after   B took down   C took from   D took off

36 There are several landladies approved by the university who take in . . . . . .
   A lodgers   B residents   C inhabitants   D settlers

37 This . . . . . of dog is very useful for hunting.
   A tribe   B stock   C clan   D breed

38 He shook hands with his . . . . . before the match.
   A opposition   B opponent   C contestant   D competitor

39 If you don't put the cheese in the refrigerator, it may . . . . . .
   A go out   B go off   C go wrong   D go over

40 She . . . . . us because she went to an expensive school.
   A looks above   B looks over   C looks down on   D looks up to

For each of the following phrases, four suggested explanations of the meaning are given, only one of which is correct. Choose the correct one.

41 I'll let you off
   A I'll help you to escape
   B I won't punish you
   C I'll take you off the field
   D I'll leave you outside

42 I can't help thinking about it
   A Nothing I do will make any difference
   B I wish I could forget it, but I can't
   C It would be more useful if I did something
   D I wish I could keep my mind on the subject

43 He's out for a profit
    A He's interested in getting money
    B He's not going to make any money
    C He's abroad on business
    D He's doing it for nothing

44 He can hardly argue with that suggestion
    A There may be a terrible row about it
    B He'll have plenty of objections to make to it
    C There is no reason for him to disagree
    D He may have a better plan of his own

45 On the other hand, he may be right
    A On the contrary, what he says is correct
    B He's correct from another point of view
    C But it's also possible that what he says is correct
    D Not at all. He's the most suitable man for the job.

In each case, there is one word with the same sound as the word given in capital letters but with different spelling. Choose which one of the four definitions given defines this word correctly.

Example: STALK
    A fixed
    B *a bird* (stork)
    C compartment for an animal
    D supply in store

46 PAIR
    A structure built out into the sea
    B a fruit
    C animal's foot
    D tiny opening in the skin

47 PALE
    A bucket
    B things put on top of each other
    C friend
    D outer skin of fruit

48 RAISE
    A go up
    B running competition
    C grain eaten in China
    D beams of light

49 MADE
    A crazy
    B one of a pair of animals
    C woman servant
    D small carpet

50 SAUCE
    A painful parts of the body
    B starting point of a river
    C stretches of land beside the sea
    D works with needle and thread

Test 450 D

Choose the correct answer. Only one answer is correct.

When dawn came, they realised that the entire boat was encased in ice. The captain ..1.. asleep but the rest of the crew hurriedly woke him. He took a small axe and with great care, ..2.. a hole in the deck, he began to knock the ice away. From time to time a wave burst over the boat and swept over him but he kept ..3.. for ten minutes while the others looked ..4.. anxiously. ..5.. this time he was so cold that he could no longer trust his grip or balance.

Each member of the crew took it in turn to cut the ice away for ..6.. he could ..7.. it. First, they had to knock off enough ice to get on their ..8... Standing up on that rolling deck ..9.. committing suicide because a man who had fallen ..10.. could not have been rescued.

Then the Captain discovered that ice was forming inside the cabin. He called to one of the crew and together they managed to get the stove ..11.. in the hope that it would ..12.. enough heat to warm the cabin above ..13.....14.. the ice in the bottom could be melted enough ..15.. pumped out, they were ..16.. danger of sinking.

It took ..17.. before the boat began to float better. But ..18.. this time they succeeded ..19.. most of the ice.

Throughout the afternoon, the coating of ice began to build up again ..20.. their work. ..21.. this new danger, Capt. Slater decided that there was too much ..22.. to gamble on the chance that the boat ..23.. until the next morning. ..24.., he ..25.. the ice. Then they settled down to wait for another day.

1 A had gone
   B had fallen
   C had become
   D had grown
	5 A By
	   B For
	   C In
	   D At

2 A so as not to do
   B for not making
   C for not doing
   D so as not to make
	6 A so long as
	   B as long as
	   C so far as
	   D as far as

3 A to work
   B to working
   C on working
   D on work
	7 A support
	   B help
	   C bear
	   D put up

4 A at
   B on
   C by him
   D for him
	8 A legs
	   B ankles
	   C knees
	   D thighs

9 A had been
   B would have been
   C had to be
   D should be

10 A overboard
   B at sea
   C to sea
   D out of board

11 A on fire
   B in flames
   C lighting
   D alight

12 A get out
   B give off
   C get over
   D give in

13 A low temperature
   B ice point
   C frozen point
   D freezing point

14 A Instead
   B In case
   C Unless
   D If not

15 A so that it could be
   B so that it would be
   C in order that it would
      be
   D for being

16 A under
   B with
   C in
   D on

17 A an hour work
   B an hour's work
   C the work of an hour
   D a work hour

18 A meanwhile
   B since
   C for
   D during

19 A to take off
   B in disposing
   C in getting rid of
   D to remove

20 A in spite of
   B although
   C whatever
   D nevertheless

21 A In front of
   B Beside
   C In the face of
   D Against

22 A on risk
   B at play
   C in trial
   D at stake

23 A would outlive
   B would survive
   C should survive
   D should outlive

24 A Another time
   B One more time
   C Once more
   D Now and again

25 A ordered that the crew
      cleared
   B suggested to the crew
      to clear
   C suggested the crew
      clearing
   D ordered the crew to
      clear

Choose the correct answer. Only one answer is correct.

26 The starter gave the . . . . . for the race to begin.
   A advice   B signal   C despatch   D attention

27 He's a nice dog. He won't do you any . . . . .
   A ill   B bite   C hurt   D harm

28 It wasn't an accident. He did it on . . . . .
   A reason   B determination   C purpose   D intention

29 We want him to retire but he won't . . . . . to it.
   A accept   B admit   C agree   D allow

30 She put a . . . . . of icing on top of the cake
   A level   B plain   C cover   D layer

31 One of the water . . . . . has burst and the kitchen is full of water.
   A tubes   B pipes   C conductors   D channels

32 A . . . . . of mine, my cousin John, has a house near there.
   A relative   B relationship   C familiar   D parent

33 I . . . . . of his course of action, so I told him to go ahead.
   A accepted   B agreed   C approved   D consented

34 Close the door please. I don't like sitting in a . . . . . .
   A blow   B draught   C vent   D current

35 There's no beer left and the pubs are shut so you'll have to . . . . . .
   A go for   B go off   C go without   D go through

36 He lost his . . . . . and hit me.
   A mood   B temper   C sense   D manner

37 At the beginning of the school year, every teacher is . . . . . a classroom.
   A allocated   B distributed   C sorted   D registered

38 She's such an irritating woman. I don't know how you can . . . . . her.
   A put up   B put up with   C stand up with   D stand with

39 He . . . . . a sum of money every week for his old age.
   A sets up   B sets in   C sets along   D sets aside

40 He fell in love with her at first . . . . . .
   A scene   B sight   C view   D look

For each of the following phrases, four suggested explanations of the meaning are given, only one of which is correct. Choose the correct one.

41 We have something in common
   A We're partners
   B We're both ordinary
   C We like each other
   D In one way, we're similar

42 The wedding's off
   A The marriage has been cancelled
   B The marriage ceremony has started
   C The bride and bridegroom are on their way to the honeymoon
   D They are going to get a divorce

43 I'm fed up with it
   A I've had enough to eat
   B I'm getting fat
   C I'm tired of it
   D I'm worn out

44 That's all for the best
   A Everything about it is perfect
   B It's finished happily in spite of everything
   C The others will have to wait their turn
   D It's an advantage, under the circumstances

45 I wouldn't take it for granted
   A I'd prefer to pay for it
   B I wouldn't assume that it will be all right
   C I wouldn't accept it at any price
   D I don't trust it

In each case, there is one word with the same sound as the word given in capital letters but with different spelling. Choose which one of the four definitions given defines this word correctly.

Example: STALK
   A fixed
   B *a bird* (stork)
   C compartment for an animal
   D supply in store

46 PRAISE
   A awarded to winner of competition
   B sum of money for which something is sold
   C speaks to God
   D pushes steadily against

47 FAIR
   A terror
   B soft hair covering some animals
   C giving heat
   D money charged for journey

48 PASTE
   A walked with regular steps
   B opposite of future
   C annoying animal or insect
   D stopped for a moment

49 STEAL
   A not moving
   B way of writing
   C metal
   D way of getting through or over fence

50 SIGHT
   A place where something is being built
   B breathed out in relief
   C place to sit down
   D one surface of an object

Test 500 A

Choose the correct answer. Only one answer is correct.

To suggest that a creative writer, in a time of conflict, must split his life into two compartments, may seem defeatist or frivolous; . .1. . I do not see . .2. . . To lock yourself up in the . .3. . is impossible and undesirable. To yield subjectively, not merely to a party machine, . .4. . to a group ideology, is to destroy yourself as a writer. We feel this dilemma to be a painful one, because we see . .5. . in politics while also seeing . .6. . a dirty degrading business it is. And most of us still have a lingering belief that if a thing is necessary it is also right. We should, I think, . .7. . this belief, . .8. . the nursery. In politics one can never do more than decide which is the . .9 of two evils, and there are some situations from which one can only escape by acting . .10. . a devil or a lunatic. War, for example, may be necessary, but it is certainly not right. Even a general election is not exactly a pleasant or . .11. . . If you have to . .12. . – and I think you do have to – then you also have to keep part of . .13. . inviolate. For most people the problem does not . .14. . in the same . .15. . , because their lives are split already. They are truly alive only in their . .16. . , and there is . .17. . emotional connection between their work and their political activities. . .18. . generally asked, in the name of political loyalty, to debase themselves as workers. The artist, and especially the writer, is asked . .19. . – in fact, it is . .20. . politicians ever ask of him. If he refuses, that does not mean that he is condemned to inactivity. One half of him, which . .21. . is . .22. . , can act as resolutely, even as violently if need be, as anyone else. But his writings, . .23. . they have any value, will always be the products of the saner self that . .24. . , records the things that are done and admits their necessity, but refuses to be deceived as to their true nature.

1 A but in the reality
   B yet in practice
   C however by fact
   D nevertheless in the
      actuality

2 A another thing he may
      do
   B what else is to do
   C what else he can do
   D another thing he
      should do

3 A fine palace
   B upstairs room
   C castle in Spain
   D ivory tower

4 A and also
   B but even
   C and just
   D but too

5 A the need to engage
   B the necessity for
      involving
   C the need to take place
   D the necessity of
      belonging

6 A what
   B how
   C such
   D as

7 A dispose
   B relegate
   C get rid of
   D extract

8 A that is of
   B which belongs to
   C that belongs to
   D which is of

9 A less
   B lesser
   C least
   D fewer

10 A as
   B such as
   C like
   D similar to

11 A edifying spectacle
   B instructing observa-
     tion
   C educating sight
   D educative view

12 A take part in such
     things
   B enter in things as
     these
   C take place in such
     things
   D involve in things as
     these

13 A you
   B one's self
   C one
   D yourself

14 A raise
   B rise
   C arise
   D arouse

15 A type
   B form
   C condition
   D style

16 A leisure hours
   B pleasure time
   C free weeks
   D hobby time

17 A never
   B none
   C any
   D no

18 A Nor they are
   B Nor are they
   C They are neither
   D Neither they are

19 A often that
   B even this
   C sometimes this
   D just that

20 A the only what
   B the only thing that
   C the only thing as
   D the only which

21 A in a meaning
   B in a sense
   C of a meaning
   D of a sense

22 A the all of him
   B all him
   C the whole of him
   D the whole him

23 A to the point
   B until
   C in so far as
   D up to

24 A sits up
   B stands aside
   C runs away
   D walks apart

Choose the correct answer. Only one answer is correct.

25 This test . . . . . a number of multiple-choice questions.
   A composes of   B composes in   C consists of   D consists in

26 There could have been a war over it but in the end reason . . . . . .
   A induced   B counted   C survived   D prevailed

27 They have asked us to . . . . . in the negotiations.
   A involve   B be mixed   C participate   D take place

28 I . . . . . on seeing the manager. The service in this hotel is terrible.
   A insist   B persist   C affirm   D protest

29 I caught a . . . . . of the car before it disappeared around the bend.
   A glance   B glimpse   C glare   D gleam

30 Would you please . . . . . from smoking while the lecture is in progress?
   A avoid   B refrain   C stop   D keep yourself

31 The country needs a . . . . . government. We have had three Prime Ministers in a year.
   A stationary   B changeless   C constant   D stable

32 A sergeant in the army wears three . . . . . on his arm.
   A stripes   B streaks   C strips   D scratches

33 Hot metal . . . . . as it grows cooler.
   A reduces   B condenses   C compresses   D contracts

34 He . . . . . a very busy life.
   A leads   B follows   C carries   D runs

35 He . . . . . the money out of my hand and ran away.
   A clutched   B snatched   C gripped   D withdrew

36 I was unable to . . . . . him to do as I said.
   A dispose   B prevail   C persuade   D convince

37 He thinks about nothing but playing golf. He's completely . . . . . to it.
   A addicted   B ascribed   C tempted   D overcome

38 I'm going into the garden to . . . . . some flowers.
   A grip   B seize   C snatch   D pick

39 We finally . . . . . an agreement after a lot of hard bargaining.
   A reached   B arrived   C did   D drove

40 He accidentally . . . . . fire to the house.
   A put   B set   C gave   D started

41 He's always . . . . . the Government but he never votes in the elections.
   A calling out   B calling off   C running down   D running out

42 The factory has increased its . . . . . by 10 per cent this year.
   A product   B output   C make-up   D exposure

Choose the correct answer. Only one answer is correct.

43 He . . . . . when his mother died
   A fell in bits   B split up
   C went to pieces   D broke himself up

44 We've spent so much money recently that our bank balance must be . . . . . .
   A in the column   B in the pink   C in the rut   D in the red

45 We've had a lot of problems to solve but at last we're . . . . . .
  A out of the wood
  C over the traces
  B up the wall
  D beyond the pale

46 He's sometimes bad-tempered but he's a good fellow . . . . . .
  A in heart   B with heart   C at heart   D by heart

In each case, there is one word with the same sound as the word given in capital letters but with different spelling. Choose which one of the four definitions given defines this word correctly.

Example: STALK
  A fixed
  B *a bird* (Stork)
  C compartment for an animal
  D supply in store

47 BROOD
  A made beer
  B red liquid
  C wide
  D stupid, animal-like person

48 LED
  A permit
  B young boy
  C go first
  D heavy metal

49 WEARS
  A not as good as
  B thin pieces of metal drawn out like thread
  C articles offered for sale
  D walls built across rivers to control flow of water

50 COURSE
  A reason for something occurring
  B savage dogs
  C rough in manners or language
  D word or phrase calling down misfortune on another person

Test 500 B

Choose the correct answer. Only one answer is correct.

The claim that a society "can teach only the values that it has" ..1.. that these values are widely recognized and ..2.. stated easily. In some societies, this is true, at least ..3... But in a free society, values are continually forming, evolving, emerging into consciousness. If we say, for instance, that the twin sources of Western civilisation are still, ..4.. all the modern changes, Christianity and the classics, that does not close the discussion. It opens it. ..5.. these broad outlines, we are no nearer to answering the enormous number of questions thrust on us by ..6.., ..7.. all resolve themselves into one basic question: ..8.. that our values are these, how do we apply them in this situation? For liberal democracy, ..9.. some other forms of government, has no answer book; we do not claim that there are ..10.. to the truth. And this, of course, puts a great strain on the teacher. In our kind of society, the teacher – ..11.. kind of teacher, from kindergarten to graduate school – is in an almost impossible position. In a society ..12.. to be sceptical about the practical use of education, except ..13.. it channels ..14.. into well-paid jobs, the teacher, who has no well-paid job, has to stand as a witness that education does confer riches and happiness. ..15.. modest he is, sooner or later he has to ..16.., "I have something to give your children. It will not ..17.. them big incomes and ..18..; it will not solve their immediate personal problems. But I am offering it, and I ..19.. accept it on their behalf." And if society, ..20.. sceptical, with an eye on the teacher's ..21.., few possessions, modest living quarters, answers with the sneer "You mean it will make them ..22.. you?", then the teacher must find within himself, somewhere, the courage to say "Yes." And not ..23... Conscious as he is of his ..24.. inadequacies and limitations, he must nevertheless appear before the world as the representative of the free human mind. It is an almost impossible demand to make of anyone. And yet thousands accept it, and undertake the impossible, in every free country.

1 A implicates
  B implies
  C infers
  D includes

2 A are capable to be
  B are possible to be
  C can be
  D are able to be

3 A to refer to the official values
  B as it concerns the official values
  C as far as the official values are concerned
  D in referring the official values

4 A although
  B nevertheless
  C however
  D in spite of

5 A At noting
  B With noting
  C Having noted
  D Having to note

6 A the actual life
  B nowadays life
  C each day's life
  D day-to-day life

7 A that
  B what
  C who
  D which

8 A put
  B given
  C expected
  D presumed

9 A not like
  B not as
  C unlike
  D different to

10 A by-passes
  B side streets
  C short cuts
  D blind alleys

11 A all
  B some
  C both
  D any

12 A inclined
  B leant
  C bent
  D probable

13 A to the point
  B for
  C in so far as
  D up to

14 A the youngs
  B the young
  C the young persons
  D the teenage

15 A It doesn't mind how
  B For
  C However
  D Though

16 A claim them
  B make the claim
  C state them
  D do the statement

17 A promote
  B fetch
  C bring
  D reserve

18 A security
  B the assurance
  C insurance
  D the safety

19 A warn you that you
  B advertise you to
  C prevent you that you
  D advise you to

20 A yet
  B still
  C once
  D no longer

21 A little profits
  B poor benefits
  C mean gain
  D low salary

22 A to be more as
  B to be more like
  C more as
  D more like

23 A take it to heart
  B set his heart on it
  C have a heart for it
  D be after his own heart

24 A self
  B proper
  C own
  D person's

Choose the correct answer. Only one answer is correct.

25 The author of the report is well . . . . . with the problems in the hospital because he has been working there for many years.
    A acquainted   B informed   C enlightened   D advised

26 The garden has been . . . . . . There are weeds growing everywhere.
    A neglected   B uncared   C miscarried   D unnoticed

27 Naturally my client will . . . . . payment of the cheque until he is satisfied that the work has been properly carried out.
    A hold in   B withdraw   C uphold   D withhold

28 I will never . . . . . them to take the child away from me.
    A let   B tolerate   C allow   D admit

29 Petrol was . . . . . and had to be rationed.
    A inadequate   B little   C lacked   D scarce

30 She is so . . . . . that she believes everything she is told.
    A frank   B naive   C sincere   D ingenious

31 These continual . . . . . in temperature make it impossible to decide what to wear.
    A transformations B fluctuations   C exchanges   D agitations

32 She's the most . . . . . secretary I've ever had.
    A efficient   B industrial   C working   D practised

33 This kind of question can sometimes be answered only by process of . . . . . .
    A abolition   B subtraction   C elimination   D exception

34 The boxer . . . . . and almost fell when his opponent hit him.
    A shattered   B scrambled   C stammered   D staggered

35 That door . . . . . when you open it. You must put some oil on the hinges.
    A rumbles   B creaks   C rustles   D cracks

36 He was . . . . . of deciding anything for himself.
    A incapable   B ineffective   C incompetent   D unable

37 He seems to think the plan will work but I am . . . . . about its success.
    A cynical   B unbelievable   C sceptical   D incredible

38 It would be . . . . . a risk to let the child go to school by himself.
    A following   B passing   C running   D carrying

39 You're old enough to . . . . . your own living.
    A win   B maintain   C gain   D earn

40 He took some money out and put his . . . . . back in his inside pocket.
    A briefcase   B wallet   C compact   D cash box

41 The actor forgot his lines but . . . . . so well that the audience didn't notice.
    A carried it off   B put it off   C went off with it   D came across it

42 She did her work quite well but she was so . . . . . that she told the boss she could run the company better herself.
    A outstanding   B outstretched   C uplifted   D outspoken

Choose the correct answer. Only one answer is correct.

43 Don't . . . . . because you're losing the argument.
   A change the subject   B alter the theme
   C pull the wool   D vary the tune

44 I can't remember the title of it exactly. I've got it . . . . . .
   A down in the mouth   B on the point of my tongue
   C at the edge of my mouth   D on the tip of my tongue

45 The children are very well, except for Emma. She's been . . . . . these last two days.
   A off health   B out of condition   C off colour   D out of the weather

46 We had given ourselves so little time to get to the airport that it was . . . . . whether we would catch the plane.
   A give and take   B touch and go   C stop and go   D to and fro

In each case, there is one word with the same sound as the word given in capital letters but with different spelling. Choose which one of the four definitions given defines this word correctly.

Example: STALK
          A fixed
          B *a bird* (stork)
          C compartment for an animal
          D supply in store

47 PEERS
   A make a hole with a sharp instrument
   B sets of two things of the same kind
   C structures built out into the sea
   D makes a noise like a cat

48 AIR
   A anger
   B person receiving title or property on the death of another
   C animal like a rabbit
   D pay for the use of something for a time

49 MINER
   A more lacking in generosity
   B way of behaving
   C more important
   D less important

50 HALL
   A opening in the ground
   B throw
   C pull with effort
   D entire

Test 500 C

Choose the correct answer. Only one answer is correct.

The appeal of the world of . . 1 . . is first its freedom. The child is compelled to go to school; he is . . 2 . . of authority. . . 3 . . to school may be decided for him. As he grows up, he sees . . 4 . . free of school and to be able to choose his job and change it if he doesn't like it, to have money in his pocket and freedom to come and go as he wishes in the world. The boys and girls, a year or two older than he is, . . 5 . . he has long observed, revisit school utterly transformed and apparently mature. Suddenly masters and mistresses seem . . 6 . . as his parents and the authority of school a ridiculous thing. At the moment the adult world may appear . . 7 . . the school world that the hunger to enter it . . 8 . . by exercises in school books, or talk of the qualifying examinations necessary for entry into professions or into the more attractive occupations. This may not be the . . 9 . . but it is a necessary part of growing up, for every man and woman must come sooner or later . . 10 . . saying "Really, I've had . . 11 . . ; I must . . 12 . . ." Some . . 13 . . , maturing rapidly because of outside influences, come to this decision . . 14 . . . Yet in a way this is not a bad frame of mind to be in . . 15 . . leaving school. At work, the young man makes one of the first great acceptances of life – he accepts the discipline of the material or the process he is working with. "The job must be done" in accord with some inexorable process he cannot alter. He . . 16 . . of it and . . 17 . . . . 18 . . life. The work process constitutes a reality in some sense superior to that of school, and this is why he so often longs to . . 19 . . it. Nothing done in school imposes its will in . . 20 . . the same way; if it is wet games can be cancelled; if the maths master is ill one can . . 21 . . . But even the boy delivering papers, . . 22 . . the driver taking out his bus, discovers that one cannot . . 23 . . because there is snow on the ground, or the foreman is irritable, or he himself . . 24 . . that morning.

1 A the work
  B work
  C the job
  D the labour

2 A under the thumb
  B below the hands
  C subject to the palm
  D in the fingers

3 A Just what he wears
  B Still what he carries
  C Even what he wears
  D Only what he carries

4 A the thing that is being
  B the being
  C what thing it is to be
  D what it is to be

5 A that
  B whom
  C which
  D what

6 A so out of date
  B as out of date
  C so out of the time
  D as out of the time

7 A so much more real than
  B so much realer than
  C so much more actual than
  D so far more in fact than

8 A may not be fed
  B cannot feed
  C may not appease
  D cannot be appeased

9 A wiser attitude
B most wise attitude
C wiser of attitudes
D wisest of attitudes

10 A up to
B until
C to the point of
D as far as

11 A enough to be learned
B enough of being
taught
C too much to be taught
D too much of being
learned

12 A do a real work
B make a real job
C make a proper work
D do a proper job

13 A young people
B youth
C youngs
D teenage

14 A too soon than they
should
B as soon as they would
C sooner than they
ought
D more soon than they
have to

15 A at the
B in
C on
D with the

16 A sees the point
B recognises the end
C agrees the use
D views the value

17 A on doing thus
B at doing that
C in doing so
D by doing like this

18 A puts himself to agree
with
B makes terms to
C goes to an agreement
with
D comes to terms with

19 A shake hands with
B get to grips with
C reach a hand to
D arrive to grasp

20 A rather
B enough
C even
D quite

21 A continue another
thing
B carry out other things
C get on with something
else
D follow some other
thing

22 A like
B as
C similar than
D the same that

23 A get it over
B put it off
C replace it
D postdate it

24 A is in a bad mood
B has a bad temper
C has the bad humour
D has lost his mood

Choose the correct answer. Only one answer is correct.

25 We'll . . . . . you as soon as we have any further information.
    A relate   B notify   C communicate   D make known

26 I'm sorry to . . . . . you while you're working but I must ask you a question.
    A intrude   B interfere   C bother   D molest

27 She's very pretty but that kind of face doesn't . . . . . to me.
    A appeal   B call   C attract   D fancy

28 All cars made nowadays are . . . . . with safety belts.
    A prepared   B packed   C built in   D equipped

29 She made it . . . . . that she didn't approve by throwing something at me.
    A plain   B sincere   C frank   D revealed

30 It was the only . . . . . of action left to me.
    A conduct   B direction   C course   D route

31 They're going to build a big office block on that . . . . . piece of land.
    A void   B blank   C vacant   D hollow

32 The company has made the usual . . . . . preliminary offer to the workers, but they won't accept it unless there is a clear statement of the new wage rates.
    A apprehensive   B suggestive   C probationary   D tentative

33 The thieves . . . . . the papers all over the room while they were searching for the money.
    A strayed   B sowed   C scattered   D broadcast

34 I didn't notice the log on the ground and . . . . . over it.
    A crept   B skipped   C stumbled   D crushed

35 The prince . . . . . power on the death of his father.
    A presumed   B assumed   C resumed   D consumed

36 Give me a . . . . . of paper and I'll write down the main points of the lecture.
    A fragment   B sheet   C blade   D leaf

37 I have promised to help you and I will . . . . . my word.
    A hold   B follow   C keep   D stick

38 He's the kind of man who's fond of . . . . . compliments to other men's wives.
    A paying   B saying   C expressing   D showing

39 I put the milk . . . . . back in the 'fridge.
    A vase   B flask   C jug   D holder

40 The lawyer will . . . . . the contract for you.
    A draw out   B do up   C do out   D draw up

41 He's . . . . . drink and never does a stroke of work.
    A gone to   B taken to   C taken up   D gone for

42 There has been a serious . . . . . of the disease in the North.
    A outbreak   B output   C outcome   D outrage

Choose the correct answer. Only one answer is correct.

43 We've been sitting here doing nothing about it for days. It's time we . . . . . the problem.
    A shook hands with   B got to grips with
    C got to brass tacks with   D reached the bottom of

44 He couldn't have meant it seriously. He must have been . . . . . .
    A twisting your arm   B pulling your leg
    C taking the sense   D doing his little joke

45 He'll never commit himself. He'll just . . . . . until everyone else has given his opinion.
    A hide under the table   B wait in the rain
    C sleep in the shadow   D sit on the fence

46 We had not been on good terms for some time but the matter . . . . . when he accused me of stealing.
    A went to my head   B came to a head
    C went out of my head   D came under this head

In each case, there is one word with the same sound as the word given in capital letters but with different spelling. Choose which one of the four definitions given defines this word correctly.

Example: STALK
               A fixed
               B *a bird* (stork)
               C compartment for an animal
               D supply in store

47 HAIR
    A person receiving title or property on death of another
    B animal like a rabbit
    C pay for the use of something for a time
    D extending further upwards

48 LEAST
    A rented
    B number of names written down
    C for fear that
    D fastened

49 HOLE
    A pull with effort
    B entire
    C throw
    D cry like a wolf

50 PAUSE
    A people without much money
    B faculties
    C used for carrying money
    D animals' feet

Test 500 D

Choose the correct answer. Only one answer is correct.

The readers of the ..1.. press are clearly not only working-class people, though working-class people must form the majority ..2.. because they are a majority of the total population. ..3.. these journals realise that the biggest single group they can aim at is ..4.. the large proportion of the population who leave school ..5.. at the age of sixteen. The scholarship system introduced after the second World War ..6.. the working classes. It is of course important not to confuse the intellectual minority ..7.. the earnest minority: a sense of social purpose need not accompany the possession of brains. Nor do all those who enjoy advanced education abandon their social class emotionally or physically. Nevertheless the intellectual minority used to stay within the working class more than it does ..8.. ..9.. members were able to improve the status of all working-class people because they were ..10.. who could meet the managers in other classes ..11.., that of the intellect. The scholarship system meant that many working-class children left their social class by a process of education. The ..12.. of middle-class children may have made it ..13.. scholarships; and a few working-class children ..14.. ..15.., or had to leave school early ..16.. financial pressure. But most of them went to grammar schools and a substantial proportion ..17.. them left their social class. Few people regretted that clever children in the working-classes had a greater ..18.. posts appropriate to their abilities. But even if the term "working-classes" is not used, ..19.. a great body of people who have to perform the more mechanical jobs. We must therefore ..20.. the fact that they are now likely to include a smaller proportion of the critically-minded than before. And this is happening ..21.. a time when those who seek the money and favour of working-people know ..22.. and have sophisticated market research at hand to help them. We must be on our guard against developing a new kind of class system, ..23.. but at least ..24.. the old.

1 A more ordinary
  B commoner
  C more popular
  D most people's

2 A specially
  B naturally
  C even
  D if only

3 A Likely
  B No doubt
  C Sure
  D Perhaps

4 A that composing
  B the which composes
  C that comprising
  D the which comprises

5 A for good
  B for always
  C definitely
  D for their life

6 A can have had an effect on
  B may have had an effect on
  C can have affected to
  D may have affected to

7 A with
  B for
  C to
  D from

8　A　in these days
　　B　in the present time
　　C　nowadays
　　D　at our time

9　A　Its
　　B　Their
　　C　His
　　D　Her

10　A　among few
　　B　among the few
　　C　of a few
　　D　of some few

11　A　in their proper ground
　　B　on their own ground
　　C　in their own land
　　D　on their proper land

12　A　home background
　　B　household
　　C　house conditions
　　D　familiar support

13　A　to be easier that they
　　　won
　　B　to be easier for them
　　　to win
　　C　easier that they won
　　D　easier for them to win

14　A　yet might not
　　B　yet could not
　　C　might not still
　　D　still could not

15　A　get them up
　　B　make them up
　　C　take them up
　　D　put them up

16　A　because of
　　B　for
　　C　for the reason of
　　D　due that

17　A　out of
　　B　of
　　C　from
　　D　between

18　A　chance of obtaining
　　B　occasion to obtain
　　C　probability for getting
　　D　possibility to get

19　A　exist
　　B　there exists
　　C　it exists
　　D　exists

20　A　take in mind
　　B　carry in mind
　　C　take into account
　　D　carry into account

21　A　through
　　B　on
　　C　at
　　D　in

22　A　to appeal them
　　B　to attract them
　　C　how to appeal them
　　D　how to attract them

23　A　one based on literacy
　　B　which one is based on
　　　literacy
　　C　a based-on-literacy
　　　one
　　D　one with literacy base

24　A　so solid as
　　B　as solid like
　　C　as firm as
　　D　so firm as

Choose the correct answer. Only one answer is correct.

25 The workers . . . . . a fair wage for their work.
   A asked   B campaigned   C appealed   D demanded

26 I . . . . . of the way he behaved at the meeting.
   A disapproved   B condemned   C disagreed   D objected

27 I can . . . . . him to you for the job. He is a very good worker.
   A suggest   B recommend   C advise   D prompt

28 He is looking for a job that will give him greater . . . . . for initiative.
   A place   B scope   C space   D suitability

29 His test results are not very . . . . . . He does well one week and badly the next.
   A invariable   B consequent   C continuous   D consistent

30 You cannot expect people to work hard unless you give them some kind of . . . . . .
   A fascination   B incentive   C provocation   D temptation

31 She is so . . . . . that she cried for days when her pet rabbit died.
   A sensitive   B sensible   C touched   D impressive

32 We must . . . . . that the telegram arrives in time.
   A secure   B ensure   C assure   D certify

33 "You didn't seriously think that she'd marry someone with your prospects and accent,
   did you?" he . . . . . .
   A sneered   B derided   C cheered   D despised

34 The man . . . . . because he had a bad leg.
   A limped   B crept   C crawled   D stuttered

35 I'm afraid this painting is not by Picasso. It's only a copy and so it's . . . . . .
   A priceless   B invaluable   C unworthy   D worthless

36 They are obviously brothers. The likeness is . . . . . .
   A infallible   B unmistakable   C faultless   D doubtless

37 It was dark in the tunnel so he . . . . . a match.
   A burnt   B struck   C fired   D hit

38 He is always . . . . . fault with other people though he doesn't do his own work properly.
   A seeking   B looking for   C putting   D finding

39 The shepherd trained the dog to look after his . . . . . of sheep.
   A flock   B pack   C herd   D collection

40 How many of you are . . . . . the Proficiency examination?
   A putting down in   B going in for
   C entering into   D writing in for

41 They were so far away that I couldn't . . . . . their faces clearly.
   A see through   B make up   C see over   D make out

42 At first everything went well with the project but recently we have had a number of . . . . .
   with the machines.
   A outbreaks   B outputs   C setbacks   D set-ups

Choose the correct answer. Only one answer is correct.

43 What a strange animal! It looks like a . . . . . a deer and a moose.

    A mix of   B result from   C half of   D cross between

44 I have . . . . . with you. Why didn't you keep your appointment with me yesterday?

    A an argument to make   B a bone to pick
    C a row to share   D a leg to pull

45 You'd better . . . . . when you speak to the boss. He's in a very bad mood this morning.

    A put your foot in it   B watch your step
    C steal a march   D mind your pace

46 Children are likely to get . . . . . if no one cares about their upbringing.

    A away from the hand   B out of the hand
    C out of hand   D away from hand

In each case, there is one word with the same sound as the word given in capital letters but with different spelling. Choose which one of the four definitions given defines this word correctly.

Example: STALK
    A fixed
    B *a bird* (stork)
    C compartment for an animal
    D supply in store

47 SEES
    A stop
    B take hold of
    C expresses sadness or relief
    D speaks words

48 SEWN
    A planted in ground or soil
    B male child
    C before long
    D cut with a saw

49 THROUGH
    A long, open box for animals to drink from
    B propelled through the air by strength of arm
    C not false
    D propel through the air by strength of arm

50 GUEST
    A sudden rush of wind
    B spirit of dead person
    C person who entertains people in his house
    D formed an opinion based on supposition